Find Me!

I'm shaped like a fan. You can find me on a beach. I start with the letter s. Can you guess what I am? Color each one of me on this page.

How many did you find?

Do you see an ice-cream cone? Draw a line to connect it with another object that rhymes with *cone*.

Seeing Double

Each object in this Hidden Pictures® puzzle is hidden twice—once in each scene.

Which vegetables are yellow? Which are orange?

cloud   wishbone   umbrella   cane   tennis ball   cork

KINDERGARTEN
K
AGES 5–6

Thinking and Reasoning
Learning Fun Workbook

For information about permission to reproduce selections from this book for
an entire school or school district, please contact permissions@highlights.com.

Published by Highlights Learning • 815 Church Street • Honesdale, Pennsylvania 18431
ISBN: 978-1-68437-285-0
Mfg. 11/2018
Printed in Beauceville, Québec, Canada
First edition
10 9 8 7 6 5 4 3 2 1

For assistance in the preparation of this book, the editors would like to thank:
Vanessa Maldonado, MSEd; MS Literacy Ed. K–12; Reading/LA Consultant Cert.; K–5 Literacy Instructional Coach
Kristin Ward, MS Curriculum, Instruction, and Assessment; K–5 Mathematics Instructional Coach
Jump Start Press, Inc.

Fish Tales

Find and circle the **5** objects in this Hidden Pictures® puzzle.

bread

saw

comb

screwdriver

doughnut

Where do you think the fish are going?

Visual Discrimination; Figure-Ground Perception

The 2 corks are circled. Can you find the rest?

Which of these items would you like to wear? Why?

starfish   drinking glass   pencil   flower   lizard   elf's hat

Ready, Set, Bowl!

Roll the ball from Start to Finish to help Anna knock down all the pins and get a strike!

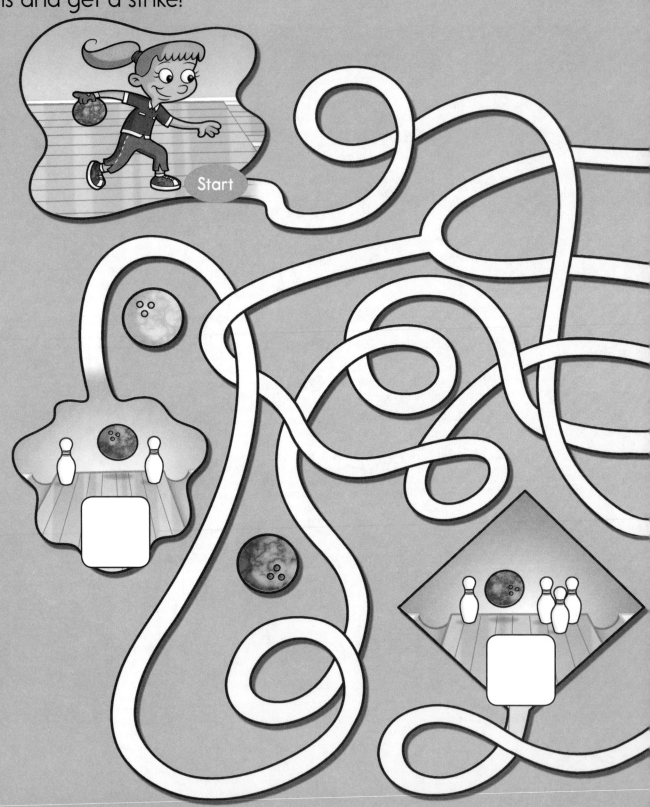

Visual Perception; Fine Motor Skills

How many pins are in each small picture? Write the number in each box.

Finish

Funny Fish

Is that a jellyfish wearing shoes? What other silly things do you see in the picture?

Circle all the fish that are blue.

Expressive Language; Fantasy/Reality

What is one silly thing you would add to this picture?

Spring on the Farm

Circle the differences you see between these pictures.

Which object in the picture is a circle?

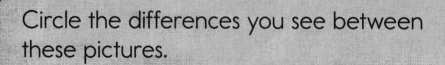

Similarities/Differences; Attention to Details

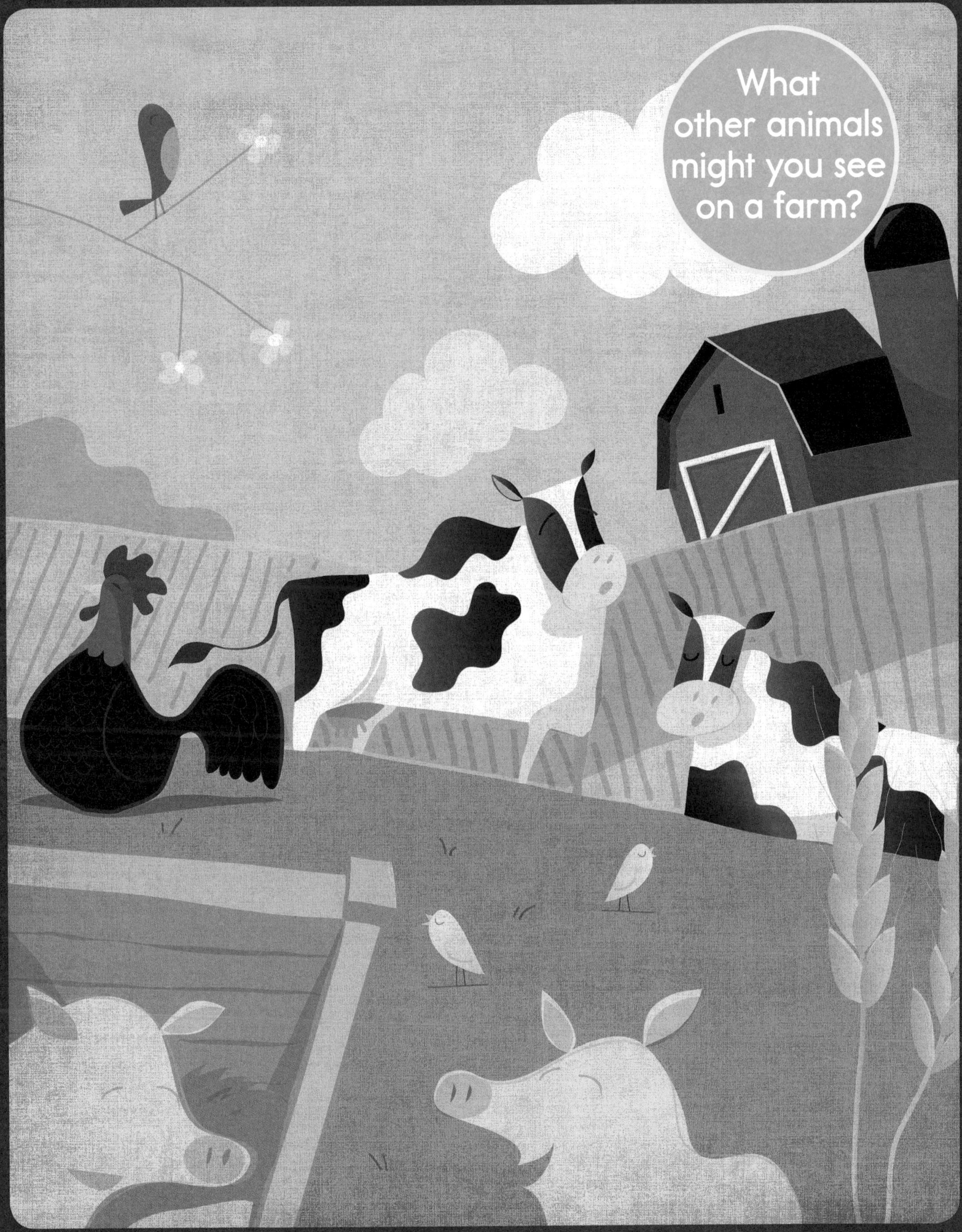
What other animals might you see on a farm?

Rinse and Repeat

How many buckets do you see? Are there more red buckets or blue buckets?

Similarities/Differences; Attention to Details

These kids are raising money for a trip. Can you find at least 15 differences between the two pictures?

What Is It?

Can you guess what this picture is?

Complete this sentence: I see

_____

- - - - - - - - - - - - - - - - - - -

_____

_____

- - - - - - - - - - - - - - - - - - -

_____.

_____

Wiggle Pictures

These insects have been twisted and turned. Can you figure out what each one is?

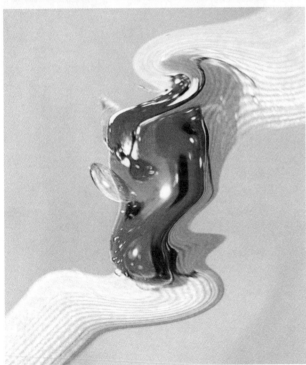

How are the insects on this page alike? How are they different?

Match Maker

Every plane in the picture has one that looks just like it. Find all 10 matching pairs.

How many planes are there in all?

Look at the 4 planes that are mostly white. How could you change one pair to make it match the other pair?

Food Code

There are **3** food jokes on the next page. Use the food code below to fill in the letters and finish the jokes.

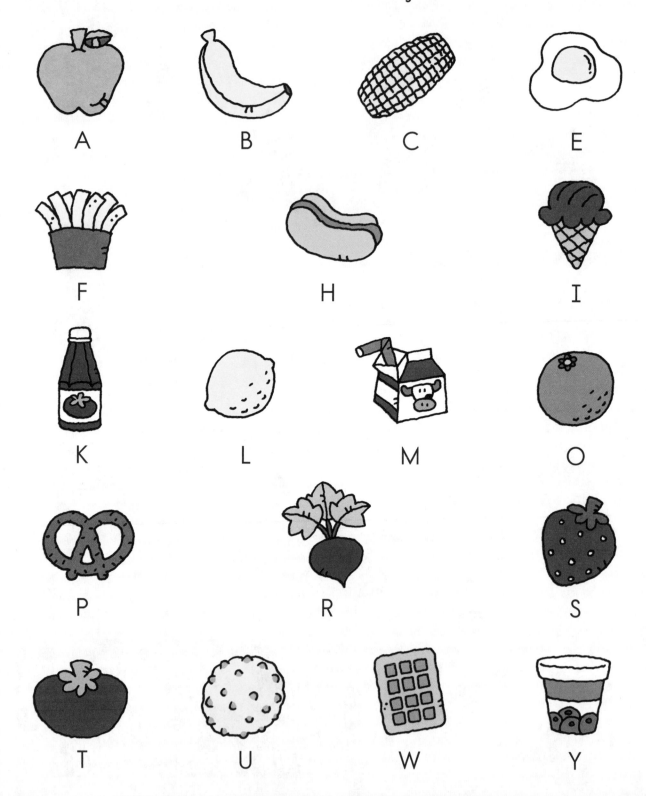

Vocabulary; Logic

What did the mustard say during the race?

"

___ ___ ___ ___ ___

___ ___ ___ ___ ___ ___ ___ ___ ___ "

Why did the cookie see a doctor?

___ ___ ___ ___ ___ ___

___ ___ ___ ___ ___ ___ .

How do you fix a broken pizza?

___ ___ ___ ___ ___ ___ ___ ___ ___ ___

___ ___ ___ ___ ___

How could you sort these foods into groups?

19

Who Painted This?

One of Mr. Brush's students forgot to put his or her name on this painting in art class today. Look at the paint colors on each easel tray to figure out who painted the picture.

Find 6 paintbrushes in the scene.

Logical Reasoning and Problem Solving

Home Sweet Home

Zig, Vot, and Spo have had a nice visit on Earth, but now they're homesick. Use the clues to help each of them get back to the right planet on the right spaceship.

Use the chart to keep track of your answers.
Put an **X** in each box that can't be true and an **O** in boxes that match.

	Hot Planet	Cold Planet	Wet Planet	Red Ship	Yellow Ship	Blue Ship
Zig						
Vot						
Spo						

CLUES:
1. Vot's planet is cold, but not wet.
2. The red spaceship came from a hot planet.
3. The yellow spaceship belongs to Spo.

Look at the word *homesick*. What two smaller words make up the word? What do the words mean? What do you think *homesick* means?

All Mixed Up

Each box shows 1 item, but the parts of the item are scrambled. Can you figure out what each item is?

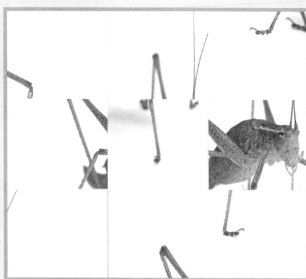

Think about the name of each item. How are the names alike?

Fruit Fun

Each picture is a close-up of a fruit. Can you tell what each one is?

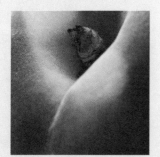  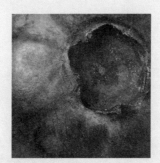 

Scientists are always making new fruits. For example, if you combine a **plum** and an **apricot**, you get a **pluot**. Think about combining a **strawberry** and a **pineapple**. Draw a picture of a **strawbapple** here.

Count the seeds on each watermelon slice. Which 2 slices have the same number of seeds?

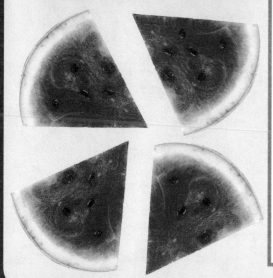

Shadow Match

These kids traced their shadows. Figure out which shadow belongs to each kid. Write the number of the shadow next to the correct kid.

How could you make a shadow on a wall? How could you change its size?

Shape Recognition; Visual Perception

Find the Shapes

Find and circle each shape in the picture below.

Which shape is purple? Which shape is brown?

Finish the Pictures

These shapes make up a puzzle called a **tangram**. The shapes in the tangram were used to make each picture below.

Each picture is missing 2 shapes. Which shapes from the tangram above do you need to finish the pictures? Color in each empty shape to match the tangram.

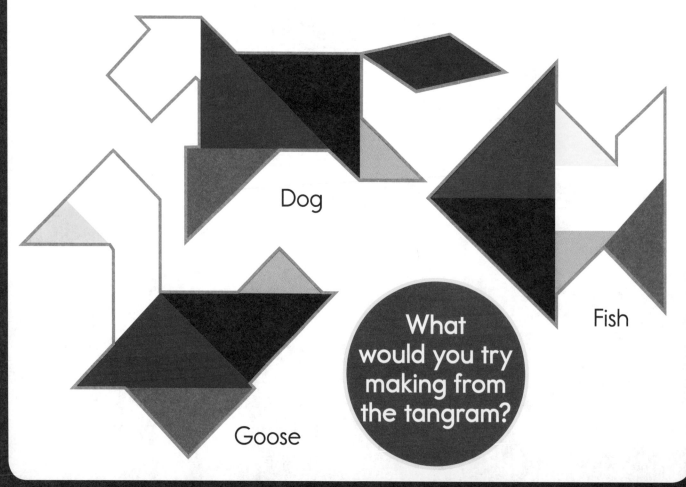

Dog

Fish

What would you try making from the tangram?

Goose

Visual Discrimination; Shape Recognition

Picture Puzzler

Cam Chameleon is playing hide-and-seek with her friends. How many hiding chameleons can you find?

How many types of flowers do you see? Which is your favorite?

What Comes Next?

Circle what comes next in each pattern.

How are the animals on this page alike? How are they different?

Back to the Barn

Help Daisy the Cow get to the barn. Follow this pattern from Start to Finish.

How many shapes are yellow? Cross off as you count.

How many are red?

Are there more yellow shapes or red shapes?

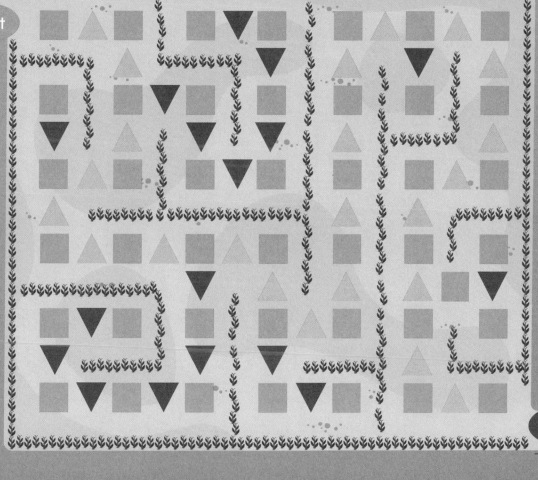

Start

Finish

Bear's Kitchen

Bear is on her way to the grocery store. Follow the directions below to help her see what food she already has.

1. Draw a square around the honey jar on the shelf.
2. Put an **X** on the banana that is not in the bunch.
3. Draw a circle around the purple fruit that is in the bowl.

Count the grapes in the bowl. Count the raspberries in the bowl. Put an **X** on the group that has more.

Position Words; Following Directions

In My Room

Follow the directions below to help Ben find the items in his room.

1. Draw a circle around the ball that is above the bed.
2. Draw a square around the object that is next to the sailboat.
3. Put an **X** on the hat that is on the bed.
4. Draw a line under the toy that is in front of the dresser.

How many triangles do you see?

Opposite Day

Find each pair of opposites.
Draw a line to match each pair.

What silly things do you see?

asleep

hot

awake

cold

many

closed

open

What Doesn't Belong?

Put an **X** on the object in each group that doesn't belong.

What are some words that rhyme with *ball*?

What are some words that rhyme with *hat*?

Visual Discrimination; Logic

What Doesn't Belong?

Put an **X** on the shape in each group that doesn't belong.

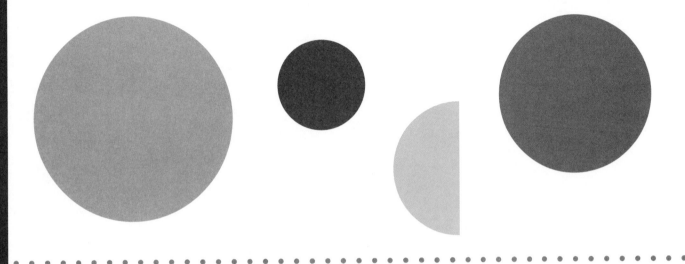

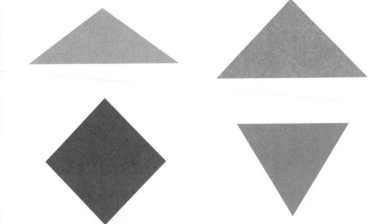

Look at the shape you crossed out in each group. What is the shape? Why doesn't it belong with the others?

How Do They Relate?

Look at the objects in the first pair. Tell how they are related. Then circle the object that completes the second pair in a similar way.

 **is to**

as  **is to** [?]

Which piece of clothing has stripes?

A.    B.    C.

- -

 **is to**

as  **is to** [?]

A.    B.    C.

How Do They Relate?

Look at the objects in the first pair. Tell how they are related. Then circle the object that completes the second pair in a similar way.

is to

as   is to   ?

A.   B.   C.

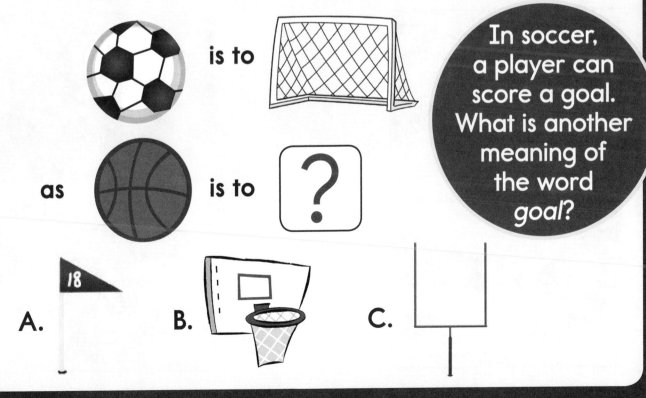

is to

as   is to   ?

In soccer, a player can score a goal. What is another meaning of the word *goal*?

A.   B.   C.

Cause and Effect

A **cause** tells why something happened. An **effect** is what happens. **Cause:** Spot was hungry. **Effect:** So Spot ate dinner. Draw a line to match each cause to its effect.

What Is the Effect?

Cause: Goofus acts up in class when he has a substitute teacher. What might happen as a result?

Draw a picture of a possible **effect**, or tell about one.

It's Time for Bed

These pictures are all mixed up. Put them in order to show how Mama Llama and her babies go home and get ready for bed. Use 1, 2, 3, and 4 to show the order.

What is your favorite bedtime book or song?

Identify, Explain Sequence of Events

Lost Dog

These pictures are all mixed up. Put them in order to show how Ted finds his lost dog. Use **1**, **2**, **3**, and **4** to show the order.

Have you ever found something you lost? How did you find it?

A Garden in the City

What do you see people doing here?

Why might people enjoy helping with a community garden?

How are gardens different from other places plants grow? How are they the same?

If you had a garden, what would you plant in it?

Try 5

1. Name 2 words that rhyme with "tug."

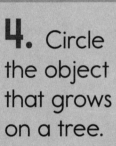

2. Name 3 animals that might live in trees.

3. Name 3 foods that are crunchy.

4. Circle the object that grows on a tree.

5. Name 3 animals that are black and white.

Batter Up!

This player on the red team is about to hit the ball. Draw a picture to show what happens next.

Why is it important for players on a team to work together?

Art Gallery

Draw a picture to show your favorite thing to do.

Read your writing to someone. Tell more about your favorite thing to do.

Write about your drawing.

Congratulations!

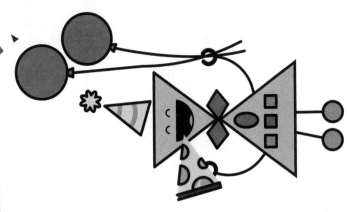

_____
(your name)

worked hard
and finished the

Thinking and Reasoning

Learning Fun Workbook

Answers

Inside
Front Cover

Daisy will eat the chocolate
ice-cream cone.

Corey will eat the strawberry
ice-cream cone.

Blake wll eat the vanilla
ice-cream cone.

Page 2
Fish Tales

Pages 4–5
Seeing Double

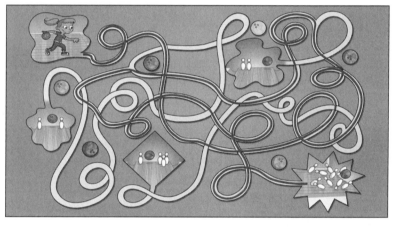

Pages 6–7
Read, Set, Bowl!

Pages 10–11
Spring on the Farm

Pages 12–13
Rinse and Repeat

There are 5 buckets.
There are more red buckets.

Page 14
What Is It?

Answers

Page 15
Wiggle Pictures

Pages 16–17
Matchmaker

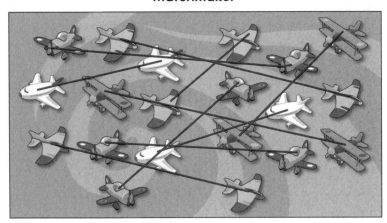

There are 20 planes in all.

Page 19
Food Code

What did the mustard say during the race?
"TRY TO KETCHUP."

Why did the cookie see a doctor?
IT FELT CRUMBY.

How do you fix a broken pizza?
WITH TOMATO PASTE

Page 21
Home Sweet Home

	Hot Planet	Cold Planet	Wet Planet	Red Ship	Yellow Ship	Blue Ship
Zig	O	X	X	O	X	X
Vot	X	O	X	X	X	O
Spo	X	X	O	X	O	X

Zig lives on a hot planet and has a red ship. Vot lives on a cold planet and has a blue ship. Spo lives on a wet planet and has a yellow ship.

Page 20
Who Painted This?

David painted the picture.

Page 22
All Mixed Up

The objects in the pictures all have names with double "p": apple, hippo, grashopper, and puppy.

Page 23
Fruit Fun

PEACH

STRAWBERRY

BLUEBERRY

PINEAPPLE

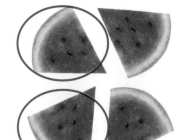

Page 24
Shadow Match

1. WILL   2. OMAR   3. AISHA   4. DAN   5. HAILEY   6. GIA   7. KELLY   8. MIKE